© 2003 by Barbour Publishing, Inc.

ISBN 1-59310-128-7

Cover image © Comstock

Published by Humble Creek, P.O. Box 719, Uhrichsville, Ohio 44683

Printed in China.
5 4 3 2 1

A CELEBRATION OF
Love

KAREN MOORE

HUMBLECREEK
INSPIRATION FOR LIFE

Let's celebrate love, the gift of joy that stimulates the soul,

stretches the heart, and creates memories for a lifetime.

Love sweeps us off our feet and carries us along

on wings of delight. . . .

Love weaves its way

into our lives,

curls up with us at home,

and keeps us warm....

Love creates our dreams,

inspires our thoughts,

and treasures our

moments....

Love celebrates

every aspect of life with us

and brings us closer to God.

Love Is a Great Thing!

*L*ove is a good thing in every way; it alone lightens what is heavy, and leads smoothly over all roughness. For it carries a burden without being burdened, and makes every bitter thing sweet and tasty. Love wants to be lifted up, not held back by anything low. Love wants to be free and far from all worldly desires, so that its inner vision may not be dimmed and good fortune bind it or misfortune cast it down. Nothing is sweeter than love; nothing stronger, nothing higher, nothing wider; nothing happier, nothing fuller, nothing better in heaven and earth; for love is born of God, and can find rest only in God, beyond all created things.

THOMAS Á KEMPIS

Love indeed is light from heaven;
a spark of that immortal fire.

LORD BYRON

Peas in a Pod

Like peas in a pod, or a hand in a glove. . .
you fit me so well, it must be love!

Happiness

The happiness of life is made up of minute fractions—the little, soon-forgotten charities of a kiss or smile, a kind look, a heartfelt compliment, and the countless infinitesimals of pleasurable and genial feeling.

SAMUEL TAYLOR COLERIDGE

"You are as majestic as the morning sky—

glorious as the moon—

blinding as the sun! Your charms are more

powerful than all the stars above."

SONG OF SONGS 6:10 CEV

*Love
is always
heart-shaped!*

Be Still My Heart

Out of the depths of my happy heart wells a great tide of

love and prayer for this priceless treasure that is confided to

my life-long keeping. You cannot see its intangible waves as

they flow toward you, darling,

but in these lines you will hear, as it were,

the distant beating of its surf.

MARK TWAIN

The passion of love bursting into flame

is more powerful than death,

stronger than the grave.

Love cannot be drowned by oceans or floods;

it cannot be bought, no matter what is offered.

SONG OF SONGS 8:6–7 CEV

Dance with the Moon

I offered the moon my arm
    and we danced
    over the crescent hills
    and lavender fields.
We sprinkled stardust
    on the meadows
    and watched the world
    shimmer in the melody
    and share our song.
It was a night for lovers,
    and we were a starstruck pair,
    soulmates of the universe
    ready to enjoy
    each other's gifts.

KAREN MOORE

One never

loves enough.

ALDOUS HUXLEY

We are tied with heartstrings.

No presents wrap me more

with love than your presence!

One finds love not by being loved, but by loving. We can never know love if we try to draw others to ourselves; nor can we find it by centering our love in them. For love is infinite; it is never ours to create. We can only channel it from its source in Infinity to all whom we meet.

J. DONALD WALTERS

Insomuch as love grows in you,

so in you beauty grows.

For love is the beauty of the soul.

ST. AUGUSTINE

Elusive Love

Elusive love on winged flight,

Lands softly to my left and right.

Perhaps if I sit quietly,

It will yet come and land on me.

KAREN MOORE

Loving Words

When loving words
    Fall through the air
Like scattered leaves
    Blown everywhere,
They warm the heart
    And for awhile
They catch the breeze
    And bring a smile.

KAREN MOORE

What is love?

Love is something like the clouds that were in the sky before the sun came out. . . . You cannot touch the clouds, you know; but you feel the rain and know how glad the flowers and the thirsty earth are to have it after a hot day. You cannot touch love either; but you feel the sweetness that it pours into everything. Without love you would not be happy or want to play.

HELEN KELLER

In real love,

you want the other person's good.

In romantic love, you want the other person.

MARGARET ANDERSON

You Are My Love and My Song

You are the song,

I will sing you forever,

You are the reason

That my life will never

Be simply another sad story.

For God heard our cries

And filled us with cheer,

And nothing can change

The things we hold dear,

And to Him we indeed

owe the glory!

KAREN MOORE

Holding On to Love

Sometimes you can stare at it boldly,

even call it by name,

and still not hold it forever. . .

love, the elusive one.

The Love Rules

- Love your partner as you love yourself, and yourself as you love your partner.

- Love so much that you will do everything to fulfill your heart's dreams and desires.

- Love others so that you seek only their good and their joy.

- Let love guide your decisions.

- Love with integrity.

❤ Be forgiving.

❤ Play.

❤ Trust that God has your life so carefully cradled in His hand that nothing can happen without His blessing. . .even love.

❤ Know that of all the "right" partners you could have, one will easily fit, like a hand in a glove. . .warm and snug.

❤ Love everyone you care about as though it's for a lifetime, because it just may be.

Love is the poetry of the senses.

It is the key to all that is

great in your destiny.

HONORÉ DE BALZAC

*W*hether modern love lasts or not is less a matter of law or religion than of continuing mutual love and respect—which now depends, perhaps more than ever, on the personal virtue of each partner.

Real love is a force more formidable than any other. It is invisible—it cannot be seen or measured, yet it is powerful enough to transform you in a moment, and offer you more joy than any material possession could.

BARBARA DE ANGELIS

Love is not only an emotion, but also a human quality, as impossible to deny as are truthfulness or courage.

Love does not dominate;

it cultivates.

JOHANN WOLFGANG VON GOETHE

In the best kind of love, both partners need and protect, give and receive. . .and admit to doing so.

Those who love deeply never grow old;

they may die of old age,

but they die young.

SIR ARTHUR WING PINERO

Love is a canvas furnished by Nature
and embroidered by imagination.

VOLTAIRE

The most wonderful of all things in life, I believe, is the discovery of another human being with whom one's relationship has a glowing depth, beauty, and joy as the years increase. This inner progressiveness of love between two human beings is a most marvelous thing, it cannot be found by looking for it or by passionately wishing for it. It is a sort of Divine accident.

SIR HUGH WALPOLE

Where there is love, there is a trinity: a lover, a beloved, and a spring of love.

ST. AUGUSTINE

A soul enkindled with love is a gentle, meek, humble, and patient soul.

JOHN OF THE CROSS

When love speaks,

the heart always listens.

Love does not exist in gazing at each other,

but in looking outward together

in the same direction.

ANTOINE DE SAINT-EXUPERY

What is the beginning? Love.
What is the course, Love still.
What the goal. The goal is love.
On a happy hill.
Is there nothing then but Love?
Search we sky or earth
There is nothing out of Love
Hath perpetual worth:
All things flag but only Love,
All things fail and flee,
There is nothing left but Love
Worth you and me.

CHRISTINA ROSSETTI

It is difficult to define love.

But we may say that in the soul, it is a ruling passion;

in the mind, it is a close sympathy and affinity;

in the body, a wholly secret and

delicate longing to possess what we love—

and this after much mystery.

FRANÇOIS DE LA ROCHEFOUCAULD

*W*hat if I could speak all languages of humans and of angels? If I did not love others, I would be nothing more than a noisy gong or a clanging cymbal. What if I could prophesy and understand all secrets and all knowledge? And what if I had faith that moved mountains? I would be nothing, unless I loved others. What if I gave away all that I owned and let myself be burned alive? I would gain nothing, unless I loved others. Love is kind and patient, never jealous, boastful, proud, or rude. Love isn't selfish or quick tempered. It doesn't keep a record of wrongs that others do. Love rejoices in the truth, but not in evil. Love is always supportive, loyal, hopeful, and trusting. Love never fails!

1 CORINTHIANS 13:1–8 CEV

Love does not make

the world go round.

Love is what

makes the ride worthwhile.

FRANKLIN P. JONES

The goal of this command is love,
which comes from a pure heart
and a good conscience and a sincere faith.

1 TIMOTHY 1:5 NIV

Your life and my life flow

into each other as wave flows into wave,

and unless there is peace and joy and freedom for you,

there can be no real peace or joy or freedom for me.

To see reality—not as we expect it to be but as it is—

is to see that unless we live for each other

and in and through each other,

we do not really live very satisfactorily;

that there can really be life only where there really is,

in just this sense, love.

FREDERICK BUECHNER

Why I Love You

I love you,

not only for what you are,

but for what I am when I am with you.

I love you,

not only for what you have made of yourself,

but for what you are making of me.

ROY CROFT
(Best Loved Poems of the American People)